Nine Fruits *of the* Spirit

A Bible Study on Developing Christian Character

Joy

Robert Strand

New Leaf Press

A Division of New Leaf Publishing Group

First printing: June 1999
Third printing: September 2009

ISBN-13: 978-0-89221-462-4
ISBN: 0-89221-462-7
Library of Congress Number: 99-64008

Cover by Janell Robertson

Printed in China

Please visit our website for other great titles:
www.newleafpress.net

For information regarding author interviews, please contact the publicity department at (870) 438-5288.

Contents

Introduction

There is an ancient story out of the Middle East which tells of three merchants crossing the desert. They were traveling at night in the darkness to avoid the heat of the day. As they were crossing over a dry creek bed, a loud attention-demanding voice out of the darkness commanded them to stop. They were then ordered to get down off their camels, stoop down and pick up pebbles from the creek bed, and put them into their pockets.

Immediately after doing as they had been commanded, they were then told to leave that place and continue until dawn before they stopped to set up camp. This mysterious voice told them that in the morning they would be both sad and happy. Understandably shaken, they obeyed the voice and traveled on through the rest of the night without stopping. When morning dawned, these three merchants anxiously looked into their pockets. Instead of finding the pebbles as expected, there were precious jewels! And, they were both happy and sad. Happy that they had picked up some of the pebbles, but sad because they hadn't gathered more when they had the opportunity.

This fable expresses how many of us feel about the treasures of God's Word. There is coming a day when we will be thrilled because we have absorbed as much as we have, but sad because we had not gleaned much more. Jewels are best shown off when held up to a bright light and slowly turned so that each polished facet can catch and reflect the light. Each of these nine jewels of character will be examined in the light of God's Word and how best to allow them to be developed in the individual life. That is how I feel about the following three verses from Paul's writings which challenge us with what their Christian character or personality should look like. Jesus Christ has boiled down a Christian's responsibility to two succinct commands: Love the Lord your God with all your heart, mind, soul, and body, and love your neighbor like yourself. Likewise, Paul the apostle has captured for us the Christian personality in nine traits:

> But the fruit of the Spirit is love, joy, peace, patience, kindness, goodness, faithfulness, gentleness, and self-control. Against such things there is no law. Those who belong to Christ Jesus have crucified the sinful nature with its passions and desires. Since we live by the Spirit, let us keep in step with the Spirit (Gal. 5:22–25).

At the very beginning of this study, I must point out a subtle, yet obvious, distinction. The "fruit" of the Spirit is a composite description of what the Christian lifestyle and character traits are all about — an unbroken whole. We can't pick only the fruit we like.

Unlocked in these nine portraits are the riches of a Christ-centered personality. The thrill of the search is ahead of us!

Joy

XAPíA, (Greek) chara,
pronounced khar-ahí,
meaning: cheerfulness, calm delight;
gladness multiplied greatly; to be
exceedingly full of joy!

THE FRUIT OF THE SPIRIT IS . . . JOY

Joyful people can be found any place and in some of the strangest of places! Being joyful is not dependent upon circumstances! Now it must be pointed out at the very beginning that

And here
is a Billy
Graham
one-liner:
"God
answers
my prayers
everywhere
except on
the golf
course."

there is a natural joy possessed by lots of people, a natural joy in the beauty of music or nature. There is a human joy in delightful relationships. There is joy in the satisfaction of a job well done. There is a healthy enjoyment of life. But we must also note that this kind of natural joy, at best, is fleeting, it's not permanent.

Sherwood Eliot Wirt was asked by Billy Graham to be the editor of a new magazine in 1958 called *Decision*. Not only was he the editor, but a warm relationship has grown between these two men over the years. "Millions of people have heard Billy Graham preach from the pulpit — but many have never heard him laugh," writes Wirt. "I can testify that he loves to laugh! At team meetings and with his family, his laughter often rings out, hearty and robust."

Wirt has written a delightful book, *Billy,* and I quote from it: "Like Nehemiah, Billy is a man of joy. The joy of the Lord is his strength; and the joy of the Lord brings laughter. He feels the joy of being alive in God's creation. He is thrilled by the prospects of future bliss in heaven."

Graham, Wirt notes, has written:

> One of the characteristics of the Christian is inward joy. Even under difficult circumstances, there will be a joyful heart and a radiant face. Unfortunately, many Christians go around with droopy faces that give no outshining glory to God. A true Christian should be relaxed and radiant, capable of illuminating and not depressing his surrounding.
>
> I have found in my travels that those who keep Heaven in view remain serene and cheerful on the darkest day. In all ages people have found it possible to maintain the spirit of joy in the hour of trial.
>
> There are times when I feel I don't have joy, and I get on my knees and say, "Lord, where is the fruit of the Spirit of joy in my life?" I find that the joy is there down deep — it is a deep river. Whatever the circumstance, there is a river of joy.[1]

WHAT REALLY IS JOY?

In your living — what are the kinds of experiences in which you have experienced real joy?

_____

_____

_____

Are joy and happiness the same thing? If not, write down the differences?

_____

_____

_____

If you believe they are the same, explain:

_____

_____

_____

The Bible has a lot to say about joy and joyfulness. Even a quick reading will give us the concept that God approves of His people being joyful. As we analyze the joy that is specifically the fruit of the Spirit, keep in mind how it can change or improve your own personal lifestyle.

Let's start our study by reading 1 Peter 1:3–9.

What has this "new birth" given to us?

_____

_____

_____

_____

Based on this text, how was it possible for these first century Christians to experience joy in spite of persecutions and even imminent death?

_____

_____

_____

_____

Are there any purposes served in suffering?

_____

_____

_____

_____

Why would God allow any of us to be hurt and suffer?

_____

_____

_____

_____

What are some of the "kinds of trials" which you have experienced?

_____

_____

_____

_____

What does the writer mean when he talks of being "refined by fire"?

_____

_____

_____

_____

_____

How would you describe "inexpressible and glorious joy"?

_____

_____

_____

_____

_____

How is it possible to be joyful in really tough circumstances?

_____

_____

_____

_____

What would this kind of joy in the middle of trial look like, act like, sound like, and feel like?

_____

_____

_____

_____

What are you currently experiencing that calls for a joyful reaction?

_____

_____

_____

_____

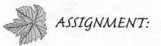 *ASSIGNMENT:*

• This study is about life situations in which joy does not come naturally. Write down one of your own tests that need joy.

_____

_____

_____

_____

_____

• Write down a plan of how you will begin to apply joy in the above situation:

_____

_____

_____

_____

_____

The word "joy" in the original Greek language means: "Cheerfulness, calm delight; gladness which is multiplied greatly." However, here in James 1:2, the word joy is modified and enhanced with the word "pure," as in "Consider it pure joy." It is the original language word, kath-ar-os, meaning "clean and clear." So an amplified version of this phrase could read: "Consider it to be clean, clear, cheerfulness, and a calm delight whenever you face trials of many kinds."

JOY IN TOUGH TIMES

There is a fascinating story out of the past which gives us an insight into an exciting bit of verse which has been set to music. Horatio Spafford had booked passage to England on a ship for his wife and four children. On this crossing in the North Atlantic, the ship ran into trouble and sank, taking his four children to a watery grave but his wife miraculously escaped drowning. As soon as it was possible, she sent a telegram to her husband with this succinct message: "SAVED ALONE." After being reunited with his wife, while on the returning voyage home, as the ship neared the place where his children had drowned, it is thought that this was the time he wrote the words that described his own grief and faith at the same time. It is one of my favorite songs and perhaps you have sung it lately:

When peace like a river attendeth my way,
　　When sorrows like sea billows roll;
Whatever my lot, Thou has taught me to say,
　　"It is well, it is well with my soul."

Though Satan should buffet, tho' trials should come,
　　Let this blest assurance control,
That Christ hath regarded my helpless estate,
　　And hath shed His own blood for my soul.

And, Lord, haste the day when the faith shall be sight,
　　The clouds be rolled back as a scroll,
The trump shall resound and the Lord shall descend.
　　"Even so" it is well with my soul.

IT IS WELL WITH MY SOUL,
IT IS WELL, IT IS WELL WITH MY SOUL.

(H.G. Spafford wrote these word in November 1873 and P.P. Bliss set them to music.)

Sorrow, hurt, and grief are the most natural reactions to tough trials and testing but from the Book of James 1:2–18 we make an exciting discovery. In the worst of times we can still say, with the help of the Spirit at work in our lives developing joy in all kinds of circumstances that it really "is well with my soul!"

What would you consider "trials of many kinds" to be which is mentioned in the "Insight" on the previous page?

_____

_____

_____

_____

_____

Why must your faith be tested?

_____

_____

_____

_____

What is a working definition of "perseverance"?

_____

_____

_____

_____

What is the relationship between "perseverance" and "maturity"?

_____

_____

_____

_____

Why is perseverance so important to your Christian lifestyle?

_____

_____

_____

_____

What is wisdom?

_____

_____

_____

_____

How does it apply to Christian living?

_____

_____

_____

_____

How does our attitude relate to perseverance, trials, and maturity?

_____

_____

_____

_____

What is the reward for people who persevere under trials and testings?

_____

_____

_____

_____

Isn't it interesting that James includes verses 13–15 which deal with temptation, in the middle of this passage on joy? Why?

_____

_____

_____

Where is the ultimate source of our joy coming from?

_____

_____

_____

Explain the significance of being "a kind of firstfruits" of His creations:

_____

_____

_____

_____

_____

_____

How do these promises in this section of the Word apply to you?

_____

_____

_____

_____

_____

_____

ASSIGNMENT:

• How have these promises of joy helped you in your current life situation?

_____

_____

_____

_____

_____

• Write out a plan of application for these truths in your life:

_____

_____

_____

_____

_____

It follows, then, does it not, that in order to fully understand a Christian's joy we must take another look at the joy-filled lifestyle of Christ. Where did His joy come from? What were the principles by which He lived?

THE JOY OF
JESUS CHRIST

I think that theologians, teachers, preachers, songwriters, artists, and authors have done a grave injustice to the average Christian. How so? Jesus Christ has been presented as a "Man of sorrows" — someone who must have been solemn and harsh and without a smile. Bruce Barton, a professional businessman had the same kind of thoughts. He felt that in order for Jesus to have been the Man of the Bible, with crowds following and little children comfortable in His presence, that something about the picture of Christ had been distorted. So he decided to reread the Gospel accounts with a clear mind and try to discover the truth about the real person of Christ. He found Him to be a Man of laughter, a Man whom children loved, women adored, and men followed. Do people want to be a dinner guest with sad-sack kind of people? Do kids want to be held by dour people? Do adults want to follow humorless leaders? Perhaps you have never read Hebrews 1:9: "You have loved righteousness and hated wickedness; therefore God, your God, has set you above your companions by anointing you with the oil of joy." His life was marked by more joy than any of his companions!

The joy of Christ consisted in doing His Father's will and work! What motivated Christ? What was of supreme importance? We don't have to be left in the dark — He told us. "My food," said Jesus, "is to do the will of him who sent me and to finish his work" (John 4:34). This was so important in His life, even more satisfying than necessary food. It was an ever-present delight. Joy came out of serving and pleasing the Heavenly Father. He said, "Here I am, I have come to do your will" (Heb. 10:9). It was a common recurring theme of His life and ministry. Joy in serving! Joy in pleasing! Joy in work!

When His work took Him in contact with the lost, there was joy in finding them, bringing them back. This is carried through in at least three parables which Jesus told — the lost sheep, the lost coin, and the lost son.

"Does he not leave the ninety-nine in the open country and go after the lost sheep until he finds it? And when he finds it, he joyfully puts it on his shoulders and goes home. Then he calls his friends and neighbors together and says, 'Rejoice with me; I have found my lost sheep' " (Luke 15:4–6).

As we read on about the lost son, we find a wonderful bottom line: "The father said to his servants, 'Quick! Bring the best robe and put it on him. Put a ring on his finger and sandals on his feet.

Christ was not only the man of sorrows, He was the epitome of joy in living! He is the ultimate example of joy in living and dying!

Bring the fattened calf and kill it. Let's have a feast and celebrate. For this son of mine was dead and is alive again; he was lost and is found.' SO THEY BEGAN TO CELEBRATE!" (Luke 15:22–24).

These three parables give us an insight into the heart of God — it's a heart that is willing to celebrate, to be joyful! It is the pure joy of God — the joy of reaching the lost, everlasting joy. No wonder Jesus was anointed with joy — He was related to His Father who is the source of joy!

There is a joy that is even deeper! How can joy be even deeper? Please consider the reaction of Jesus after He had sent the 70 followers out in ministry. I only hope that heaven has a video of this happy time. Jesus is listening to the reports of joy-filled followers upon their return following this time of ministry. Now the focus from Luke 10:21: "At that time Jesus, FULL OF JOY through the Holy Spirit. . . ."

Other translations read like this: "Jesus rejoiced in spirit — He thrilled with joy (Moffatt. "He was inspired with joy" (Phillips).

What was the specific reason? It was in the revelation of love and wisdom which the Father had hidden from the wise and learned. He rejoiced in what the Father was doing as well as taking joy in what the Father was. Jesus became joyful in His spirit as He observed and was aware of what was happening in the lives of His followers.

Then — there was the joy set ahead of Him! There was a joy still ahead. The joy He was experiencing while doing the will and work of the Father was founded or based on the certainty of a greater joy which was still ahead. There were those awful moments of travail in the garden, there was coming the agony of the cross, but most importantly, there was the joy of the Resurrection and ultimately the return to glory to be seated at the right hand of the Father who had sent Him. This was the joy in victory!

"Let us fix our eyes on Jesus, the author and perfecter of our faith, who FOR THE JOY SET BEFORE HIM endured the cross, scorning its shame, and sat down at the right hand of the throne of God. Consider Him (Heb. 12:2–3).

For Christ, while He still walked the dusty roads of this earth — the best was yet to come! In Him and in His lifestyle and ministry we have the supreme example of what real joy is all about.

C.S. Lewis wrote:

> The settled happiness and security which we all desire, God withholds from us by the very nature of the world; but joy, pleasure and merriment, He has scattered broadcast. We are never safe but we have plenty of fun and some ecstasy. It is not hard to see why. The security we crave would teach us to rest our hearts in this world and pose an obstacle to our return to God: a few moments of happy love, a landscape, a symphony, a merry meeting with our friends, a bath or a football match, have no such tendency. Our Father refreshes us on the journey with some pleasant inns but will not encourage us to mistake them for home.

THE JOY OF THE CHRISTIAN

The Bible explicitly states that the joy of Jesus Christ is to be the same kind of joy of the individual Christian! That kind of fruit-bearing depends upon relationship.

For this next study, let's read John 15:1–17.

Explain what comes to mind when you read about the vine and its branches:

_____

_____

_____

_____

Who is the "true vine"? Who is the "gardener"? And what specifically is the job of the gardener?

_____

_____

_____

_____

_____

_____

_____

What happens if you are already living a lifestyle that is bearing the fruit of joy?

_____

_____

_____

Explain what is meant by the conditional "if" as found in verse 5:

_____

_____

_____

_____

There is an "if" found in verses 5, 6, and 7. Why do you think Jesus used this conditional word so often in relationship to fruit-bearing?

_____

_____

_____

_____

What happens to the branch that does not remain connected to the true vine?

_____

_____

_____

_____

_____

Have you discovered the key to remaining in a fruit-bearing connection with the true vine? If so, explain:

_____

_____

_____

_____

_____

How are we to relate to other branches in this fruit-bearing mode?

_____

_____

_____

_____

Explain, the relationship of love to bearing the fruit of joy:

_____

_____

_____

How is it possible to bear "fruit that will last"?

_____

_____

_____

_____

What is the difference between being "friends" or being "servants"?

_____

_____

_____

_____

What is our purpose in being chosen and appointed?

_____

_____

_____

_____

And the bottom-line commandment is:

_____

_____

_____

_____

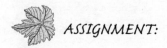 *ASSIGNMENT:*

• What can you do, personally, to strengthen the relationship with the true vine, Jesus Christ, so that joy is more fully matured in your lifestyle?

_____

_____

_____

_____

_____

• In what ways can you make a life application of the truth we have uncovered to this point?

_____

_____

_____

_____

_____

THE JOY THAT COMES FROM DOING THE WILL OF GOD

W. Beran Wolfe penned these lines:

> If you observe a really happy man you will find him building a boat, writing a symphony, educating his son, growing double dahlias in his garden, or looking for dinosaur eggs in the Gobi Desert. He will not be striving for it as a goal in itself. He will have become aware that he is happy in the course of living life twenty-four crowded hours of the day.[2]

This is the fundamental, basic joy of the Christian. Sin is a condition of not doing God's will, breaking God's laws, refusing God's will — a life of disobedience. When that person becomes a Christian, there is a new desire to do the will of God as revealed to us in our act of repentance and from our study of God's word. Life has a new focus. The bottom line to the revival in Samaria under the ministry of Philip says it all for new believers: "So there was great joy in that city" (Acts 8:8)! Further, let's take a look at Acts 13:52 where the joy of the young, beginning Christian is enriched with the Holy Spirit: "And the disciples were filled with joy and

"A rejoicing heart doeth good to the body" (YLT).

"A joyful heart worked an excellent cure" (RHM).

"A cheerful heart makes a quick recovery" (Knox).

with the Holy Spirit." There is the initial new experience, a first joy of relationship, but there are some Christians who lose it because they have refused to follow the initial beginning with a lifestyle of full surrender and obedience to God.

Many of God's choicest servants have been joyful people because of what they have discovered about serving. Oswald Chambers, the man who wrote one of the greatest daily devotionals of all time, *My Utmost for His Highest*, was known and loved for his rollicking sense of humor and joyful lifestyle. After meeting Chambers for the first time, one serious seminarian said, "I was shocked at what I then considered his undue levity. He was the most irreverent reverend I had ever met."

Charles Spurgeon of London, of much religious writing, was rebuked by a lady in his congregation for his too-frequent expressions of joy and the use of humor in his preaching. To which he replied, "Madam, you should give me a medal for holding it back as much as I do."

On one occasion, Oswald Chambers was speaking with a young soldier who told him, "I hate religious people." To which Oswald replied, "So do I." And with that issue settled and out of the way, he listened to the young man's heartbreaking story and eventually led him in a sinner's prayer of forgiveness.

Are you aware that the word "joy" in some form (i.e., joyful, joyfully, rejoicing, rejoice, etc.) appears more than 200 times in the Bible? The Bible is a book of joy! The Bible is full of people who lived a joy-filled life! Do you need strength? It's to be found in the joy of the Lord! Not only is it a book of joy, read it again and observe how often the people of God spent their days in feasting or celebrating who they were and their relationship with God.

Not only all of that — joy is therapeutic to you who might be experiencing it as well as to others who may be observing or sharing it with you. Note Proverbs 17:22: "A cheerful heart is good medicine, but a crushed spirit dries up the bones!"

The life of joy and the actions of being joyful are conveyed in such terms as delight, happiness, gladness, exultation, ecstasy, elation, excitement, cheerfulness, glee, delectation, jubilation, enjoyment, pleasure, contentment, jubilant, ecstatic, pleasing, bright, heartening, light-hearted, rapturous, merry, and delightful! WOW!

The joy that was so much a part of the living of Jesus Christ in seeking and finding that lost sheep will also be our kind of joy in service and ministry. To me, it has always been surprising how many Christians have been seeking and longing for joy in a mistaken search for a "deeper" kind of experience. It's so simple and so obvious — the joy of winning others to Christ is a joy that even the angels must envy. Christians that are sharing with others in an evangelistic outreach are happy people. Likewise soul-winning churches are joy-filled, joyful churches. It's no great mystery how being filled with joy in serving happens and how it works.

Before we go back to the Bible for our next study, let's have a bit of background so we can understand the theme of this book.

In the Book of Philippians, Paul and Timothy are telling us the secret of the joy-filled life in spite of circumstances. As we read from this passage, always keep in mind that this letter was written from a Roman dungeon, not the best of circumstances from which to be writing about joy!

Now let's read Philippians 1:3–26.

To whom is this Book of Philippians addressed?

_____

_____

_____

Why does Paul "always pray with joy"?

_____

_____

_____

_____

What kind of a relationship did Paul have with these people as noted in verses 7–8?

_____

_____

_____

How did he pray for them?

_____

_____

_____

_____

What was the key to Paul's wonderful attitude about his current circumstances of being in chains?

_____

_____

_____

_____

In verse 18, there is another reason for Paul to rejoice. What was it?

_____

_____

_____

_____

_____

_____

With what kind of an attitude was Paul facing his certain death?

_____

_____

_____

_____

_____

_____

_____

Explain in your own words the dilemma Paul was confronted with:

_____

_____

_____

_____

_____

How many times in these verses has the word joy or rejoice appeared? And how was each usage different?

_____

_____

_____

_____

_____

_____

What kind of values and desires is Paul expressing here?

_____

_____

_____

_____

What were the positive assurances that Paul was basing his joy on?

_____

_____

_____

_____

Paul is excited about the spread of the gospel. Honestly, do you have the same kind of joy over the gospel message being expanded?

_____

_____

_____

Why?

_____

_____

_____

Why not?

_____

_____

_____

ASSIGNMENT:

• In your lifestyle, what do you gravitate to for your sources of joy?

_____

_____

_____

_____

• As we have worked our way through this portion of the Word, it's obvious that Paul's joy was an all-consuming kind. Now — let's give consideration to a bottom-line kind of question: What would it take for you to experience this kind of a joyful lifestyle?

_____

_____

_____

_____

_____

JOY THAT LASTS

One of our major problems in this area is that we have focused on the wrong things, the wrong input, the wrong attitudes. We have missed what joy is all about. We have lost our focus, we have lost sight of what is important in maintaining joy and living the joyful life.

After 40 some years of married life, this lady's husband died. For several months she sat alone in her home with shades drawn and doors locked. Finally, she decided to do something about her loneliness. She went to a pet store. As she looked over the dogs, cats, fish, and even reptiles, nothing seemed right. Then the owner showed her one of his prized parrots. "Does it talk?" she asked.

"Absolutely — a real chatterbox. Friendly disposition and a wide vocabulary. That's why it's so expensive. But what a friend he could be to you."

"Sold!" She bought an elegant large cage. Took him home in anticipation. At last a companion, something to talk to — perfect. But the parrot wouldn't say a word.

She went back to the pet store and complained to the owner, "Not one word! I haven't been able to get a sound out of that bird."

"Well, you need to buy a mirror. A parrot needs a mirror so while looking at himself, he'll talk." She bought a mirror. It didn't help — not a word from the bird.

Back she went to the owner, "The parrot still isn't talking."

"Did you buy a ladder?"

"No, I didn't know it needed a ladder." She bought the ladder — but no use, the parrot still didn't talk. Then it was a bell, the next week a swing. Not one sound from the cage.

Then she suddenly burst into the pet store shouting, "It died! My expensive bird is dead at the bottom of the cage with the mirror, bell, ladder, and swing!" Oh, was she ever angry.

The owner replied, "Well, I can't believe that. I'm shocked. Did it ever say anything at all, ever?"

"Yes, as a matter of fact it did. As it lay there taking its last few breaths, it said very faintly, 'Don't they have any food down at that pet store?' "

In focusing on the right things, again, from Philippians 4:4–9, we can extrapolate six words that sum it all up:

WORRY ABOUT NOTHING

—

PRAY ABOUT EVERYTHING!

In order to do that, there are also three simple steps: Rejoice (verse 4); Relax (verse 5); Rest (verse 7)! The bondage of worry is because worry forces us to focus on the wrong things. Paul had found the secret to everlasting joy.

There is another key — Paul wrote in verse 11, "For I have learned!" It's a process of learning and living it out. He said, "I have learned!" But the real question is, "Have you learned?" Now what had he really learned? "I have learned — THE SECRET OF BEING CONTENT IN ANY AND EVERY SITUATION!" (verse 12). What a simple discovery! Simple in concept — sometimes quite difficult to work out in the real life world of reality.

In the final greetings that Paul penned is one of the most intriguing verses in all of the Bible. "All the saints send you greet-

One of the major obstacles to living the life of joy is the enemy of worry, to which God already has the answer: "Do not be anxious about anything" (Phil. 4:6).

ings, ESPECIALLY THOSE WHO BELONG TO CAESAR'S HOUSEHOLD"! (Phil. 4:22). This Caesar is the infamous Nero — the man who purportedly fiddled while Rome burned. He was the Nero who was the major persecutor of Christians — the one who threw them to the lions in the coliseum. He is the man who burned Christians at the stake. Exactly who in this household was he referring to as "saints"?

Legend tells us that while Nero was out of town, his wife listened to the message of joy Paul was proclaiming and turned her life over to Christ. When he returned he was furious. Could this have been the turning point in the decision to behead Paul?

But there must have been many others because Paul talks about saints. What happened to the soldiers who were chained to Paul — no escape for an entire watch while he joyfully talked of Jesus Christ!? What a man! What a way to live! What a way to leave this life — joyfully in spite of circumstances!

The point is that we all should be joyful, in fact it could make us laugh out loud! Jesus Christ has invaded and infiltrated the very citadel of unbelief — under Nero's nose! Therefore, my weary, joyless friend, "REJOICE IN THE LORD ALWAYS, I WILL SAY IT AGAIN: REJOICE!" (verse 4).

For our final study, please read Psalm 33:1–11, 20–22; and Matthew 28:21, 23:

Who does the Psalmist say is to sing to the Lord in praise?

_____

_____

_____

How are we to praise the Lord?

_____

_____

_____

_____

Specifically — how are praise and joy related?

_____

_____

_____

_____

_____

_____

_____

How often should we praise the Lord?

_____

_____

_____

_____

_____

Do you think it is always appropriate to praise the Lord? If so, please explain:

_____

_____

_____

_____

For what are we to praise the Lord?

_____

_____

_____

The Psalmist writes of several ways in which to praise the Lord. How should we be praising the Lord in our modern world?

_____

_____

_____

Now let's focus on our Matthew verses. What is the invitation which Christ gives all about?

_____

_____

_____

_____

_____

_____

What is the real meaning contained in the "Come to me" invitation?

_____

_____

_____

_____

_____

Explain how "rest for your souls" relates to a life of joy?

_____

_____

_____ /

_____

To what does "my yoke" refer?

_____

_____

_____

What would it mean to you personally when you have experienced
this "rest" for your individual soul?

_____

_____

_____

_____

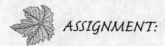 *ASSIGNMENT:*

• This short study on joy is almost completed. Now — how do you plan to implement in your life these truths which have been uncovered?

_____

_____

_____

_____

• Write a profile about how a joyful Christian will live out life:

_____

_____

_____

_____

_____

_____

IN SUMMARY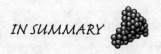

And so — perhaps, we have discovered that the joy of the Lord is the answer to living a meaningful life. It's one very important element in completing the character of a Christian. This particular fruit gives us a taste of what heaven must be like!

> And the ransomed of the Lord will return. They will enter Zion with singing: everlasting JOY will crown their heads. Gladness and joy will overtake them, and sorrow and sighing will flee away (Isa. 35:10).

David wrote that this fullness of joy is everlasting: "You have made known to me the path of life; you will fill me with joy in your presence, with eternal pleasures at your right hand" (Ps. 16:11).

Sometimes, in order for us to really understand the implication of this truth, God may allow life to strip us of all outward circumstances that would normally bring a sense of happiness so that we might focus on our relationship with Him. The classic example of this comes out of the writings of an Old Testament prophet who had apparently learned the hard way — read carefully and rejoice!

Though the fig tree does not bud and there
    are no grapes on the vines,
though the olive crop fails
    and the fields produce no food,
though there are no sheep in the pen
    and no cattle in the stalls,
YET I WILL REJOICE IN THE LORD, I
WILL BE JOYFUL IN GOD MY SAVIOR!
    (Hab. 3:17–18).

And the fruit of the Spirit is . . . JOY!

1   Sherwood Wirt, *Billy* (Wheaton, IL: Crossway Books), taken from *The Joyful Noiseletter*, Aug./Sept. 1997, p. 6, used with permission.
2   W. Beran Wolfe, *The Treasure Chest* (San Francisco, CA: Harper & Row).

Nine Fruits of the Spirit

Study Series includes

Love

Joy

Peace

Patience

Kindness

Goodness

Faithfulness

Gentleness

Self-Control

Robert Strand

Retired from a 40-year ministry career with the Assemblies of God, this "pastor's pastor" is adding to his reputation as a prolific author. The creator of the fabulously successful Moments to Give series (over one million in print), Strand travels extensively, gathering research for his books and mentoring pastors. He and his wife, Donna, live in Springfield, Missouri. They have four children.

Rev. Strand is a graduate of North Central Bible College with a degree in theology.